The Car Sales Conversation Starter Guide

How to Begin Natural Conversations That Lead to Sales

Bruce Huddleston

Bedrock Heritage Publishing

The Car Sales Conversation Starter Guide

How to Begin Natural Conversations That Lead to Sales

Copyright © 2026 by Bruce Huddleston

All rights reserved.

Published by Bedrock Heritage Publishing

A Division of Life Guidance Consulting LLC

Tyler, Texas

www.bedrockheritagepublishing.com

ISBN: 978-1-972179-15-4 (Paperback)

ISBN: 978-1-972179-68-0 (EPUB)

Car Sales Survival Guide Series — Book 7 of 10

Manufactured in the United States of America

DISCLAIMER

This book is based on the author's personal and professional experiences, observations, and opinions, accumulated over a 35-year career in the automotive industry. It is intended for educational and informational purposes only.

The stories and anecdotes contained in this book are drawn from real-world situations encountered throughout the author's career. However, names, identifying details, specific circumstances, employer names, dealership names, and individual characteristics have been changed, omitted, combined, or fictionalized to protect the privacy of the individuals involved. Any resemblance to specific living persons, current or former employers, or existing businesses is coincidental and unintentional.

No individual, dealership, organization, or employer referenced or implied in the stories within this book has reviewed, approved, or endorsed the content herein. The recollections and characterizations presented are solely the author's own perspective and memory of events and do not constitute a factual record, legal testimony, or statement of fact regarding any identifiable person or entity.

The sales strategies, techniques, and professional advice presented in this book reflect the author's personal approach and experience. Individual results will vary based on experience, effort, market conditions, dealership policies, and other factors beyond the author's control. Nothing in this book constitutes a guarantee of income, employment, or professional outcome.

The author and publisher have made reasonable efforts to ensure the accuracy of information presented at the time of writing. The author and publisher make no representations or warranties regarding the completeness, accuracy, or current applicability of the information contained herein, and expressly disclaim any liability arising from the use or application of the content of this book.

By reading this book, you acknowledge and agree that the author and publisher shall not be liable for any damages, losses, or claims arising directly or indirectly from the use of or reliance upon any information contained herein.

For the salesperson standing on the lot right now, trying to figure out what to say after hello.

Nobody handed me the words either. I learned them one conversation at a time, mostly by getting them wrong first. This book is the shortcut I wish somebody had given me.

Talk to people like people. The rest takes care of itself.

FREE BONUS FOR READERS

Your Complete Digital Script Library

Get the Car Sales Survival Quick-Reference Card — a free companion to this book that puts the key rules and techniques on one page you can keep at your desk.

Visit:

www.carsalessurvivalseries.com/scripts

Enter your email to claim your free reader bonus.
Print it. Keep it. Use it.

Contents

INTRODUCTION

Here's something nobody told me when I started.

The sale is not the close. It's not the test drive. It's not the numbers on the desk or the signature on the line. The sale is the conversation. Everything else is just what happens after the conversation has gone well.

Think about the deals you've lost. I'll bet most of them didn't fall apart over price. They fell apart in the first minute, before price ever came up, because the conversation never actually started. The customer said, "Just looking," you said, "Okay, let me know," and that was that: no conversation, no relationship, no deal.

This book is about the part of the job that comes right after the greeting. You've made your approach. You've introduced yourself. You're standing in front of a human being who came onto your lot for a reason. Now what?

Most salespeople reach for a sales question. "What are you looking for today?" "What's your budget?" "You trading something in?" Those are fine questions. They're just the wrong ones to lead with, and I'm going to spend a good part of this book explaining why.

What I want you to understand up front is this: starting a real conversation is a skill. It is not a personality trait you're either born with or not. It is not a clever line you memorize. It is a thing you can learn, practice, and get good at, the same way you got good at anything else worth doing.

And it is worth doing. The salesperson who can start a real conversation wins customers that everybody else writes off as tire-kickers. Not because they're slick. Because they're someone the customer is actually willing to talk to.

That's the whole game. Be someone worth talking to, and then give the customer a reason to talk to you. The rest of this book is how.

"The Rule: The conversation is the sale. Everything else is just paperwork."

Chapter 1

Why Most Sales Conversations Die in the First Minute

MOST CAR SALES CONVERSATIONS are dead within sixty seconds. Not because the customer wasn't serious. Not because the salesperson didn't know the product. They die because the salesperson reached for a sales question too early, and the customer did the only thing a normal person does when they feel a sales process starting before they've agreed to be in one.

They shut down.

Here's the opener that kills more deals than any other:

"What are you looking for today?"

Sounds harmless. It isn't. Think about what that question actually tells the customer. It tells them: we are now in a sales transaction. I am the salesperson. You are the prospect. Let's get to it.

The customer hasn't decided any of that yet. They just got out of their car. Maybe they're nervous. Maybe they had a bad experience at the last lot. Maybe they just want to look at a truck for ten minutes without somebody trying to qualify them. And you've just told them the clock is running.

So they say the magic words. The two words that end the conversation before it starts.

"I'm just looking."

And here's the part most salespeople get wrong. They take that personally. They think the customer is being difficult, or lying, or not a real buyer. None of that is true. "Just looking" is not a verdict on you. It's a completely honest answer to the question you asked. You asked them to step into a sales process, and they declined. That's all.

The questions that kill conversations all have one thing in common: they ask the customer to give you something before you've given them any reason to. Budget. Trade. Timeline. What they're looking for. Every one of those is you reaching into the customer's pocket in the first minute.

A real conversation runs the other direction. You give first. You're a person, they're a person, and you talk like it. The information you actually need — the budget, the trade, the timeline — comes out on its own once the customer decides you're worth talking to. It always does.

FROM THE FLOOR

I walked into a well-known furniture store one afternoon looking for a recliner. Had a specific one in mind. Knew what I wanted to spend. Ready to buy. Three salespeople were sitting on a showroom couch. I could hear them — in earshot, not trying to be quiet — debating whose turn it was to help me. Like I was an interruption to whatever they were doing.

The one who drew the short straw walked over. No greeting. No name. No smile. Just: "What are you here to buy today?"

I said: "Nothing. I'm just looking. I'll let you know if I need help."

And I meant it. They'd lost me in the first five seconds. I didn't buy a thing there. Went somewhere else and bought the same recliner the same afternoon.

The irony is, I walked in ready to spend money. All they had to do was make me feel like a person, not a chore. Instead, they spent more energy arguing over whose turn it was than they spent on the customer standing in front of them. That's not a sales problem. That's a culture problem. And it starts—and ends—with how a team treats the greeting.

I was a ready buyer. Cash in hand. And they lost me with one question, because that question told me exactly what the next twenty minutes were going to feel like.

Your customer is making the same read every time. The first thing out of your mouth answers a question they haven't asked yet: Is this going to be a hassle? Get that answer wrong, and the conversation's over before it started.

"The Rule: A sales question asked too early gets you 'just looking' — every time."

Chapter 2

Conversation Questions vs. Sales Questions

There are two kinds of questions you can ask a customer, and most salespeople never learn the difference between them. Once you do, half of this job gets easier.

A sales question is anything that asks the customer to give up information you'd use to qualify them. Budget. Trade-in. Timeline. Who the decision-maker is. What they're pre-approved for. These are working questions. You need the answers. But notice what they all have in common: each of them benefits only you. The customer gets nothing back for answering. They just feel sized up.

A conversation question is anything a person could answer comfortably while standing in line at the grocery store. Where'd you drive in from? That's a sharp-looking truck you pulled up in—how long have you had it? Kids keeping you busy this summer? Nobody tightens up answering those. There's nothing to defend.

Both kinds have a place. The mistake almost everybody makes is inverting the order. They lead with sales questions and save the conversation for later—if there is a later. By then, the customer has already decided how much of themselves they're going to share, and the answer is usually "not much."

Run it the right way around and watch what happens. Start with a conversation. Let the customer get comfortable. And here's the thing nobody believes until they've seen it: the sales information comes out on its own. The customer who wouldn't tell you their budget when you asked in the first minute will volunteer it in minute six, unprompted, because now they're talking to a person they trust instead of answering a salesperson they don't.

Here's a quick test. Before a question leaves your mouth, ask yourself: could a stranger answer this in the checkout line without feeling cornered? If so, it's a conversation question and safe to lead with. If no, it's a sales question, and it can wait until you've earned it.

You will earn it faster than you think. Customers are not stingy with information. They're stingy with information given to people who haven't earned it. Earn it first, and the rest is just listening.

"The Rule: If they couldn't answer it in the grocery line, it's not an opener."

CHAPTER 3

THE OPENER: WHAT TO SAY AFTER HELLO

I'M NOT GOING TO give you a line to memorize. If I did, you'd say it like you were reading it off a card, and the customer would hear exactly that. What I'm going to give you is the shape of a good opener so that you can build your own in your own voice.

A good opener does one job: it gives the customer an easy, no-pressure place to start talking. That's it. It is not designed to qualify them, impress them, or move them toward a vehicle. It is a door you hold open. Whether they walk through it is up to them, but you make it easy for them.

Here's the shape. You acknowledge something real, and then you get out of the way. Watch how that plays in a few different spots.

On the lot, walking up to someone looking at a truck:

"That's a good-looking one. I'm Bruce — take your time, I'll be right over here if you've got any questions."

Walk-in, somebody who just came through the showroom door out of the heat:

"Come on in out of that heat. I'm Bruce. What brought you out today — anything in particular, or just seeing what's out there?"

A return customer, somebody you recognize from a previous visit:

"Good to see you back. Last time you were looking at the SUVs, if I remember right — still thinking that direction?"

Look at what those have in common. None of them asks for a budget, trade, or timeline. Every one of them gives the customer an effortless way in and an effortless way out. "Just seeing what's out there" is a perfectly fine answer to all of them, and notice—you offered it yourself. When you hand a customer the easy exit before they have to reach for it, they seldom take it. It's when they feel trapped that they bolt.

Notice something else. The return-customer opener works because you remembered. That's not a trick. That's you having paid attention last time. The best openers aren't clever—they're specific. Specific to this customer, this vehicle, this moment.

The worst openers are generic, and customers can smell generic from across the lot, because they've heard it at every store they've been to. "What can I do to put you in a car today?" is generic. "That's the third one of those somebody's looked at this week — they're moving fast" is specific, true, and gives them something to react to.

Build a handful of openers you're comfortable with. Say them out loud until they sound like you and not like a script. Then throw the script away and just notice what's actually in front of you: the customer, the vehicle, the weather, the moment. There's always an opener sitting right there. You just have to be paying enough attention to see it.

"The Rule: An opener isn't a line you memorize. It's a door you hold open."

CHAPTER 4

FINDING COMMON GROUND WITHOUT FORCING IT

EVERY CUSTOMER BRINGS SOMETHING with them onto your lot that gives you a way in. The plate is from another state—the bumper sticker for a college, a band, or a cause. The kid is asleep in the back seat—the team logo on the hat. The work truck has a company name on the door. These aren't random. They're the things customers chose to carry into the world, which means they're usually happy to talk about.

That's common ground, and it's the easiest conversation fuel there is — when it's real.

Here's the catch, and it's a big one. There's genuine common ground, and there's the forced version, and customers can tell the difference instantly. Forced common ground is when you pretend to care about something to manufacture a connection. "Oh, you're a Cowboys fan? Me too, biggest fan, love them." If you're not, the customer knows, because the second they ask you a follow-up question, you've got nothing, and now you're a salesman who lies about small things. They will assume you lie about big ones, too.

Genuine common ground is just noticing something true and saying a true thing about it.

"Saw the plates — you drove all the way down from Colorado? That's a haul. What brings you to Texas?"

You don't have to be from Colorado. You don't have to know anything about Colorado. You just have to be a curious human being who noticed something real. That's it. Curiosity beats fake enthusiasm every time, and it's a lot less work.

The kid in the back seat is the most underused one of all. Most salespeople walk right past the kid like furniture. A parent notices everything about how you treat their child. Acknowledge the kid — a wave, a quick word, "looks like you've got a co-pilot today" — and you've told that parent something about yourself that no sales pitch could.

One rule on common ground: it's a way in, not the whole conversation. The point isn't to talk about Colorado for twenty minutes. The point is to start with something easy and real, get the customer comfortable, and let it open into why they're actually here. Common ground is the on-ramp. Don't mistake it for the highway.

And if you don't see any common ground? Don't invent it. A clean, simple, honest opener beats a forced connection every single time. When there's nothing real to comment on, just be straightforward and let the customer lead. Forcing it does more damage than skipping it.

"The Rule: Notice what they brought with them. Don't manufacture what isn't there."

CHAPTER 5

LISTENING AS A SALES SKILL

LISTENING IS THE MOST under-trained skill in this entire business. Every dealership in America will train you on the product, the process, the paperwork, and the close. Almost none of them will train you to shut up and listen. Which is a shame, because it's the one that makes all the others work.

Most salespeople don't listen. They wait. There's a difference. Waiting is when the customer is talking, and you're just standing there, loading up the thing you were going to say next, looking for the half-second gap to jump in. The customer can feel that. They can tell you are not listening the same way you can tell someone is reading their phone while you talk.

Real listening looks different, and customers notice it just as fast. You let them finish. You don't finish their sentences. When they say something that matters, you follow it instead of steering back to your agenda.

Say a customer mentions, almost in passing, that their last car left them stranded on the highway with their daughter. A salesperson who's waiting hears "needs a new car" and moves on. A salesperson who's listening hears the whole thing — the fear, the stranded daughter, the reason reliability just became the only thing that matters to this person. That one sentence told you how to sell them. But only if you heard it.

Here's a move almost nobody has the nerve to use: let the silence sit. When a customer finishes a thought, most salespeople rush to fill the quiet. Don't. Give it a beat. Nine times out of ten, the customer keeps talking, and the second thing they say is the real thing. The first answer is the polite one. The silence is what pulls out the honest one.

The salespeople whose customers tell them the most aren't the ones who talk the most. They're the listeners. The customer walks away from that conversation feeling understood, and feeling understood is most of what people actually want from anyone, salesman or not.

FROM THE FLOOR

One afternoon, a customer pulled into the lot in a taxi. That caught my attention — most people drive themselves in. This one stepped out and walked directly toward a specific vehicle, as if he already knew exactly what he was looking for.

I didn't rush. I stood up, walked out at a normal pace, and gave him a small wave as I crossed the lot. When I reached him, I introduced myself and told him I'd be glad to help if he had any questions.

He told me he'd just gotten off a flight and came straight from the airport. His vehicle was destroyed in a parking lot fire while he was traveling. He'd seen one of our ads and came directly to us. He knew which vehicle he wanted. He just needed to drive it and confirm it.

We took a short test drive. Came back. He asked how to make out the check.

Start to finish, maybe forty-five minutes. The deal was easy because the approach was right. No pressure, no assumptions, no rushing. Just a professional greeting and a willingness to follow the customer's lead.

Not every customer comes in ready to buy. But every customer deserves that same professional opening. You never know which one will be the taxi customer — the one who's already decided and just needs someone not to get in their way.

The taxi customer is the perfect example of listening as a sales skill, because the skill was almost entirely restrained. The deal was sitting right there. The only way to lose it was to start talking, start pitching, start qualifying

— to get in the way of a customer who already knew what he wanted. The salesperson listened, followed, and stayed out of the way. Forty-five minutes.

You won't get a taxi customer every day. But you'll get plenty of customers who are further along than you assume, and the only way to find out is to listen long enough to let them tell you.

"The Rule: The customer will tell you how to sell them — if you shut up long enough to hear it."

CHAPTER 6

The Bridge: From Small Talk to What They Came In For

So you've started a real conversation. The customer's relaxed, talking, comfortable. Now you've got a different problem, and it's one a lot of salespeople fumble: how do you get from the conversation to the actual reason they're here without it feeling like somebody flipped a switch?

Because that's the danger, you spend five good minutes being a human being, and then — click — you snap into salesman mode. "So anyway, what's your budget?" And just like that, the customer's guard goes right back up. They realize the conversation was the warm-up, and now the real thing is starting. You just told them the friendly part was a tactic. Everything you built, gone in one sentence.

The bridge is how you cross over without breaking the trust. And the secret is that the right bridge doesn't feel like a bridge at all. It feels like the next sentence.

Here's how it works. Somewhere in the conversation, the customer will hand you an opening—a natural pause, or better yet, something they say that connects to why they're here. Your job is to notice it and step through it gently.

Customer mentions their family has outgrown their current car. That's the bridge, right there:

"Yeah, those back seats fill up fast. Is that part of what's got you looking — needing a little more room?"

See what that did? It didn't change the subject. It followed the subject straight into the reason they came. The customer doesn't feel handed off from the friendly guy to the salesman, because it's the same guy, still listening, still following what they said. The conversation just turned a corner. It didn't stop and start over.

The wrong bridge ignores what the customer gave you and reaches for your agenda instead. The right bridge uses what they just said as the doorway. That's why listening (the last chapter) and bridging (this one) are joined at the hip. You can't build a good bridge if you aren't listening to the spot where you're putting it.

If no natural opening comes, you can build a soft one. "Well, let me ask you this —" works fine as long as the question on the other side is a gentle one, not a wall of qualifiers. Ease into the needs, don't lunge at them.

The whole thing should feel, to the customer, like one continuous conversation that drifted toward cars. Because that's exactly what it is.

"The Rule: The right bridge feels like the next sentence. The wrong one feels like a switch flipped."

CHAPTER 7

WHEN THE OPENER FALLS FLAT

IT'S GOING TO HAPPEN. You're going to deliver a perfectly good opener and get nothing back. A shrug. A one-word answer. A customer who clearly does not want to talk. The opener fell flat, and now there's an awkward little silence where the conversation was supposed to be.

Most salespeople panic here. And when a salesperson panics, they talk. They fill the silence with features, with the lot special, with whatever's nearby, anything to make the quiet stop. That's the worst thing you can do. You've now confirmed the customer's fear — that this is going to be a hard sell — and you've done it while they were already pulling back.

A flat opener is not a dead deal. It's information. It's the customer telling you something needs to change. Maybe it's the timing—they just got out of the car and need a minute. Maybe it's the approach—you came in a little too hot. Maybe they had a rough morning that has nothing to do with you. You don't always know which. But you do know the move: change something.

Sometimes the right change is to give space.

"Tell you what — I'll let you look. I'm right inside if you need me, no rush at all."

That's not giving up. That's reading the room. A customer who feels you back off the right way will often come back to you twenty minutes later, relaxed and ready to talk on their own terms. You didn't lose them. You let them set the pace, and they'll remember it.

Other times, the right change is a small acknowledgment that resets the whole thing.

FROM THE FLOOR

The summer heat in Texas is no joke. I was managing a used-car lot — no air conditioning on the lot, obviously — and it was one of those July afternoons when the asphalt is soft, and the air feels like a wet towel. A couple pulled in. I watched my newest salesperson sprint out to meet them — which was already the wrong move — and by the time he got to them, he was visibly sweating through his shirt. The customers looked at him, looked at each other, and said they were just looking. He came back inside looking defeated.

I went out. Introduced myself. Said: "Sorry about the heat — let me know if you want to step inside and cool off while we talk." That's all it took. They came inside. We sold them a car in ninety minutes. The first salesperson did everything wrong before he said a word. I did one thing right: I acknowledged where they were before I asked anything of them.

The first salesperson got a flat "just looking" and treated it like the end. It wasn't. The customers weren't closed — they were hot, uncomfortable, and being rushed by a sweating stranger. One honest line that acknowledged the situation instead of pushing past it changed everything.

That's the lesson. When the opener falls flat, stop pushing and start reading. Ask yourself what the flat response is actually telling you, change that one thing, and the conversation you thought was dead will usually start right up.

"The Rule: A flat opener isn't a dead deal. It's a cue to change something."

CHAPTER 8

Conversations with Couples and Families

S ELLING TO ONE PERSON is one conversation. Selling to a couple or a family is several conversations happening at once, and if you only have one of them, you lose.

The most common mistake is picking a person. The salesperson decides, usually in the first few seconds, who the "real" buyer is — often the husband, often whoever spoke first — and aims the whole conversation at them. Everyone else becomes an audience—big mistake. The person you wrote off as the audience is frequently the one who actually decides, and even when they're not, they have full veto power, and you just spent half an hour making them feel invisible.

Include everyone. That's the whole skill. Greet both halves of a couple, by name if you can get them. Acknowledge the kids—not as a tactic, just because ignoring a child in front of their parent is a quiet insult the parent will never quite forgive. If somebody's grown daughter came along to help her mother shop, talk to the daughter, too. She's there for a reason, and she has opinions.

Then read the room. Watch who looks at whom before answering. Watch whose face the questions get checked against. The decision-maker in a couple is often not the loud one — it's the quiet one, the loud one keeps glancing at. You find that out by paying attention to the whole group instead of locking onto one person.

Here's the thing you absolutely cannot do: play one against the other. Don't take sides in the little disagreements couples have on the lot. "Well, your husband's right, that's really the smarter buy," might win you the husband for a second, but you just made an enemy of the wife, and she remembers. Stay neutral. Stay honest with everyone in the group at once. The second person feels you're working on the other one; trust is gone for both of them.

A family that feels like you saw all of them — every person, including the kid kicking the tire — is a family that trusts you. And a family that trusts you will tell you everything you need to know, together, out loud, in front of each other. That's the easiest deal there is.

"The Rule: If one person in the group feels invisible, you've already lost the room."

CHAPTER 9

CONVERSATIONS ON THE LOT VS. INSIDE THE SHOWROOM

THE SAME CUSTOMER HAS a different conversation with you depending on where you are standing. Most salespeople use the same approach everywhere, and it ends up costing them. The lot and the showroom are different rooms, and they call for different conversations.

On the lot, you've got the world working with you and against you at the same time. There's an actual vehicle right there to talk about — you can pop a hood, open a door, and point at the truck's bed. There's endless real, concrete stuff to comment on. That's the lot's gift. The cost is that there's also weather, noise, traffic, other customers, and a hundred distractions. The customer's attention is split, and so the conversation has more material but less focus.

So on the lot, keep it moving and keep it physical. Let the vehicle do some of the talking. Walk and talk. Comment on what's in front of you. Don't try to have a deep, sit-down conversation while you're both squinting in the sun next to a busy road. The lot is for getting interested, getting comfortable, and getting a feel.

Inside the showroom, everything changes. It's quieter. You're probably going to sit down, maybe across a desk, and the second you sit down, things get more formal, whether you want them to or not. The distractions drop away. Now you've got focus—but you've lost the easy material the lot gave you. There's no truck to point at. It's just the two of you and the conversation.

So inside, slow down. Lower your register. This is where the real listening happens, where the customer will tell you the things they wouldn't say standing in a parking lot. The showroom conversation is more personal, so earn it by being more present. Don't bring a lot of energy to a showroom chair — the customer sat down to have a more serious conversation, and bouncing around like you're still outside reads as you not matching the moment.

The skill is the adjustment. Same customer, same deal, two different conversations depending on the room. Notice where you're standing, and let the room set the pace.

"The Rule: Match the conversation to the room you're standing in."

CHAPTER 10

CONVERSATIONS ON THE PHONE

ON THE PHONE, YOUR voice does it all. Every bit of work that your face, your posture, your handshake, and the lot would normally do, your voice has to carry alone. That's why the phone scares so many salespeople, and why the ones who get good at it have such an edge. Most of your competition is bad at the phone.

There are two completely different phone conversations, and you can't run them the same way.

The inbound call is a customer who picked up the phone and dialed you. They have a reason. They saw a vehicle online and have a question. The number one rule on an inbound call: do not turn into a robot. The customer can hear you stop being a person and start being a process the instant it happens.

"Thanks for calling. This is Bruce. Which one caught your eye?"

Warm, short, and it hands the conversation right back to them. Compare that to the salesperson who answers an inbound call and immediately starts demanding a name, a number, and an email before answering the one question the customer actually called to ask. That customer hangs up and calls the next store.

On an inbound call, answer the question they called with first. Be helpful before you're acquisitive. The information you want — their name, their number, getting them to come in — comes much easier once you've actually helped them with the thing they called about.

The outbound call is the opposite situation. You're calling someone who didn't expect to hear from you: a lead, a follow-up, or a previous customer. The challenge here is that you're interrupting their day, so the opening has to respect that from the start.

"Hi, this is Bruce over at the dealership — did I catch you at a bad time?"

That one question does a lot. It acknowledges that you're an interruption, it gives them an easy out, and it treats them like a person with a life instead of a name on a call sheet. Most people, given that courtesy, will give you a minute. The salespeople who barrel straight into a pitch the second someone says hello get hung up on, and they earn it.

On every phone call, inbound or out, smile while you talk. I know how that sounds. Do it anyway. It changes your voice, and your voice is the only tool you've got on the line. The customer can't see you, so the only version of you they get is the one they can hear. Make it a good one.

"The Rule: On the phone, your voice does the work your face can't. Sounds like a person."

CHAPTER II

THE CUSTOMER WHO WON'T OPEN UP

SOME CUSTOMERS WILL NOT talk. You do everything right — good approach, good opener, real common ground, genuine listening — and you still get one-word answers, crossed arms, and eyes that won't meet yours. It's the most discouraging customer there is, because it feels like rejection.

Here's the first thing you have to get into your head: it is seldom about you.

The quiet customer is usually quiet for reasons that walked in the door with them. They had a terrible experience at the last dealership. They hate buying cars and have hated it their whole life. They're nervous about the money. They're shy. They had a fight in the car on the way over. They're grieving. You have no idea what that person is carrying, and you will drive yourself crazy if you treat their silence as a review of your performance.

So don't. Treat it as information. Something needs to be adjusted, and your job is to figure out what without forcing it.

Sometimes the adjustment is to back off the pressure entirely. Give them room. Stop asking questions and just let them look, with you nearby and easy. Sometimes a customer who won't talk while they feel watched will start talking the moment they feel free.

And sometimes — this is the one nobody expects — the problem isn't the conversation at all. It's something you can't see and would never guess.

FROM THE FLOOR

I had a colleague who couldn't get any traction with a woman at the used-car lot. She kept saying she was just looking. He couldn't figure out what was off—he'd done everything right as far as he could tell. He came and got me.

I went out, introduced myself, and asked how I could help her.

She said: "God, thank you. I really want to buy this car. But that other guy looks exactly like my ex-husband, and I cannot stand the sight of him."

Nothing to do with the car. Nothing to do with the approach. She knew exactly what she wanted — she just needed a different person in front of her before she would let the conversation happen. We tested the vehicle, worked out fair numbers, and she drove home happy.

Don't take "I'm just looking" personally. Don't take it as a verdict. Take it as information — something needs to be adjusted. Sometimes that's your approach. Sometimes it's giving more space. And occasionally it's a different person entirely. All of those are workable. None of them is the end of the deal.

My colleague did everything right and still couldn't open her up, because the thing in the way had nothing to do with him and everything to do with a face he happened to share with her ex-husband. He couldn't have known. He couldn't have fixed it by trying harder. The fix was to have a different person walk out there.

That's the lesson for every quiet customer. When the conversation won't start, stop assuming you failed and start asking what the silence needs. More space. A different approach. A fresh face. A return visit on a better day. All of those are workable. None of them means the customer isn't a buyer. They just mean something has to change before the conversation can happen — and the salesperson who can sell to the quiet ones, too, has an edge most of the floor never develops.

"The Rule: Silence usually isn't about you. Don't take it personally — take it as information."

CHAPTER 12

BECOMING SOMEONE WORTH TALKING TO

EVERYTHING IN THIS BOOK so far has been technique—openers, bridges, listening, recovery. Technique matters. But there's a level above technique, and the salespeople who live up there make all of this look effortless. They've become someone customers actually want to talk to.

You can't fake that, and you can't script it. But you can build it.

Here's the uncomfortable truth: you cannot have a good conversation if you have nothing to bring to it. A salesperson who reads nothing, notices nothing, and is curious about nothing has nothing to talk about beyond cars and weather. They run out of conversation in ninety seconds, and the customer feels the bottom of that well immediately.

The salespeople who never run dry are the ones who pay attention to the world. They read books, the news, whatever. They're curious about how things work and how people tick. So when a customer mentions they just retired from teaching, or they're moving cross-country, or their kid just made the team, the salesperson actually has something real to say back, and a real follow-up question to ask. The conversation has somewhere to go because the salesperson brought it there.

Just as important is what these salespeople don't do: they don't need to win the conversation. The salesperson who has to top every story, who turns every customer comment into a story about themselves, who can't let the customer be the interesting one — that salesperson is exhausting, and customers shut down around them. Being worth talking to means being secure enough to let the other person have the floor. The customer should leave feeling like the interesting one. That only happens when you don't need to be.

Think about the salespeople you've watched lose a customer before they ever said a word about a car — frantic, self-focused, too busy performing to notice the person standing in front of them. No clever opener fixes that, because the customer has already read who they are. Being worth talking to isn't something you switch on when you reach the customer. It's who you are as you walk across the lot.

Build the habit of being a curious, present, secure person who pays attention to the world. Do that, and you'll never run out of things to talk about, and customers will feel the difference the moment you walk up. Every technique in this book works better when delivered by someone like that.

"The Rule: You can't have a good conversation if you've got nothing to bring to it.

CHAPTER 13

THE CONVERSATION STARTER TOOLKIT

THIS CHAPTER IS THE whole book on one shelf. It's meant to be read before a shift or pulled out after a rough day to reset. None of it is a script. These are patterns to understand, not lines to recite. Internalize them, then build your own from them.

Opener patterns

Acknowledge something real, then get out of the way. Comment on the vehicle, the weather, the drive in — then offer an easy way in and an easy way out in the same breath. Lead with specific, never generic. And always offer the easy exit first; they rarely take it.

Common-ground prompts

Out-of-state plate, bumper sticker, team logo, work truck, the kid in the back seat. Notice what the customer brought with them and say one true thing about it. Curiosity beats fake enthusiasm. If there's nothing real to comment on, skip it — a clean, honest opener beats a forced connection.

Conversation questions vs. sales questions

Before a question leaves your mouth: could a stranger answer this in the grocery line without feeling cornered? Yes — it's safe to lead with. No — it's a sales question, and it waits until you've earned it. You'll earn it faster than you think.

Listening cues

Let them finish. Don't finish their sentences. Follow what matters to them, rather than steering back to your agenda. And let the silence sit — the second thing they say is usually the real thing.

Bridge phrases

Use what they just said as the doorway. When they mention the reason they're here, follow it: "Is that part of what's got you looking?" The right bridge feels like the next sentence, not a switch flipping. If no natural opening comes, "Let me ask you this" works—as long as the question that follows is gentle.

Recovery moves

When the opener falls flat, stop pushing and read it. Give space: "I'll let you look, I'm right inside." Or acknowledge the situation: a single honest line about the heat, the wait, the day can reset a closed customer. A flat opener is a cue to change one thing, not a reason to quit.

The customer who won't open up

Seldom about you. Back off the pressure, give yourself some room, or recognize that the problem may be something you can't see. More space, a different approach, a fresh face, a better day — all workable, none of them the end of the deal.

"The Rule: Don't memorize the lines. Understand the patterns, and build your own."

Conclusion

After the greeting and the first impression, the entire rest of this job is one long conversation. That's the idea this whole book is built on. You can know every vehicle on the lot cold, you can be sharp on the numbers, you can have the cleanest process in the store — and none of it matters if the customer never decides to talk to you.

The salespeople who win the conversations win the customers that everybody else loses to "just looking." Not because they're slick. Because they're someone the customer was willing to open up to. They lead with conversation instead of qualification. They notice what's real instead of forcing what isn't. They listen more than they talk. They bridge gently instead of flipping a switch. And when an opener falls flat, they read it and adjust instead of pushing harder or giving up.

Every one of those is a skill, which means every one of them gets better with practice. You will not be perfect at this tomorrow. Nobody is. But you'll be better than you were, and the customer in front of you tomorrow will feel the difference even if they couldn't name it.

Talk to people like people. Be someone worth talking to, give them an easy reason to talk, and then get out of the way and listen. Do that consistently, and the deals take care of themselves. They always have.

TIPS FOR THE SALES MANAGER

If you run a floor, this chapter's for you, manager to manager.

Here's what I see in most stores: managers coach the close and ignore the conversation. They'll spend an hour drilling a salesperson on overcoming objections and not one minute on how that salesperson starts a conversation in the first place. That's backward. The objections you're drilling mostly come from conversations that started wrong. Fixing the front and the back gets easier.

Coach the opening. Get out on the floor and actually watch your people make contact with customers. Are they leading with a sales question or a conversation? Are they listening or waiting? Do they back off well when an opener falls flat, or do they panic and talk? You can't coach what you don't watch, so watch.

Use role-play, and don't let your people roll their eyes at it. Have them practice openers on each other—the lot, the walk-in, the return customer, the phone. It feels silly in the moment. It builds real reps before the reps cost you a live customer. The salesperson who's said it fifty times in practice says it like a person on deal fifty-one.

And catch them doing it right. This is the one managers skip. When a salesperson handles a conversation well — a clean recovery off a flat opener, a customer who opened up because they listened — point it out, out loud, where the rest of the floor can hear it. You reinforce the behavior in that person, and you teach it to everyone in earshot at the same time. Public praise for the right conversation is the cheapest training you'll ever run.

When the whole floor learns to start conversations instead of pitches, the whole store feels different to a customer the second they pull in. That's on you. Build it.

APPENDIX

The Rules

Every chapter in this book ends with one. Here they all are, in order, in one place.

Introduction

"The Rule: The conversation is the sale. Everything else is just paperwork."

Chapter 1

"The Rule: A sales question asked too early gets you 'just looking' — every time."

Chapter 2

"The Rule: If they couldn't answer it in the grocery line, it's not an opener."

Chapter 3

"The Rule: An opener isn't a line you memorize. It's a door you hold open."

Chapter 4

"The Rule: Notice what they brought with them. Don't manufacture what isn't there."

Chapter 5

"The Rule: The customer will tell you how to sell them — if you shut up long enough to hear it."

Chapter 6

"The Rule: The right bridge feels like the next sentence. The wrong one feels like a switch flipped."

Chapter 7

"The Rule: A flat opener isn't a dead deal. It's a cue to change something."

Chapter 8

"The Rule: If one person in the group feels invisible, you've already lost the room."

Chapter 9

"The Rule: Match the conversation to the room you're standing in."

Chapter 10

"The Rule: On the phone, your voice does the work your face can't. Sounds like a person."

Chapter 11

"The Rule: Silence usually isn't about you. Don't take it personally — take it as information."

Chapter 12

"The Rule: You can't have a good conversation if you've got nothing to bring to it."

Chapter 13

"The Rule: Don't memorize the lines. Understand the patterns, and build your own."

ALSO AVAILABLE

More from the Car Sales Survival Guide Series by Bruce Huddleston.

Book 10 — The First Five Minutes With a Car Buyer
How to Transition from Greeting to Conversation and Move Toward the Sale

Work With Bruce

If you're interested in one-on-one coaching, sales team training, or dealership consulting, Bruce works with individuals and organizations through Life Guidance Consulting.

For inquiries:

www.lifeguidanceconsulting.com

bruce@lifeguidanceconsulting.com

For publishing inquiries or bulk orders:

www.bedrockheritagepublishing.com

info@bedrockheritagepublishing.com

ABOUT THE AUTHOR

Bruce Huddleston spent thirty-five years in the automotive industry, working every level of the business from showroom floor salesperson to finance manager, sales manager, used car manager, and general manager. His career included new-car franchise dealerships, independent used-car operations, and a decade in buy-here, pay-here — giving him a breadth of experience that few in the industry can match.

He began as a high school dropout who needed a job and ended up discovering a profession. He ended as a veteran who had trained hundreds of salespeople, managed multiple departments, and built a reputation for straight talk in an industry that doesn't always reward it.

Since retiring, Bruce has opened a life coaching practice, assists his wife with her mental health therapy practice, and operates Bedrock Heritage Publishing, a division of Life Guidance Consulting LLC, where he writes practical guides for sales professionals across multiple industries.

The Complete Car Sales Survival Guide is his flagship work. The Car Sales Survival Guide Series — a collection of focused training guides on specific sales skills — is built on the same foundation of real experience, honest insight, and zero tolerance for the kind of nonsense that gives sales a bad name.

He lives in Tyler, Texas.

A Quick Favor

If The Car Sales Conversation Starter Guide helped you — if it changed how you walk onto a lot, how you read a customer, or how you think about what your body is saying before you open your mouth — I'd be grateful if you'd take two minutes to leave a review wherever you bought it.

Reviews matter more than most people realize. They help other salespeople find books that can actually make a difference in their work. And honest feedback helps me keep writing things worth reading.

You can simply scan the QR code below.

https://www.amazon.com/review/create-review/?asin=1972179152

www.bedrockheritagepublishing.com

Thank you for spending time with this book. Now go to work.

— Bruce Huddleston